LOVE STORY

A Journey of Faith, Grace, and God's
Unfailing Love

PUBLISHED BY: Erma Major Shaw

ISBN :978-1-7326812-2-4

First Edition, October 2024.

Printed in the United States of America

Disclaimer:
This book is a work of creative nonfiction. Any resemblance to actual persons, living or dead, is purely coincidental.

Table of Contents

Introduction

Every great love story captivates the heart, but this one—my love story with the Lord—transcends anything you might expect. It is a journey that began with simple prayers in childhood and has unfolded into a profound relationship that extends beyond time, into eternity. I came to author this book out of a deep desire to profess my faith and share the most important love affair of my life—the one I have with my Lord and Savior. Through every trial, every joy, and every moment in between, I have come to realize that God's love is unchanging, unconditional, and always present.

This book is not just my story—it reflects God's love and His pursuit of each of us. It is for anyone searching for answers, for hope, or for a deeper connection with their Creator. Perhaps you have faced loss, struggled with your identity, or wondered where God fits into your life. Through my individual experiences, I hope to show you that His love is always there, waiting for you to fully embrace it.

The problem this book seeks to solve is one that many of us face: the feeling of emptiness or longing that no human relationship or achievement can fill. I have learned through my own journey that only God's love can truly satisfy the deepest parts of our soul. As you read, you will discover how to recognize God's presence in your life, how to deepen your faith, and how to embrace the love that has been pursuing you all along.

I invite you to join me on this journey, not just to read my story, but to reflect on your own. Through the chapters ahead, I pray that you will find comfort, healing, and most importantly, the undeniable truth that God's love is the greatest love of all.

Chapter 1: The Beginning of Our Love Story

"Now I lay me down to sleep. I pray the Lord my soul to keep. If I die before I wake, I pray the Lord my soul to take.

God is good, God is great let me thank Him for my food, Amen.

These words were the first prayers I ever whispered, a child's simple plea for protection before sleep and gratitude before meals. At the time, I did not fully understand the depth of what I was saying, nor did I grasp to whom I was speaking. I just knew I was talking about "the Lord, and God," names that felt distant and yet familiar. Little did I realize then that the Lord, the God I spoke of so casually, had already set His love upon me long before I could even say His name. yet God, in His great love, listened intently to every word. The innocence of my childhood faith, not knowing that "the Lord" and "God" were the same deity, did not hinder my relationship. In fact, it made it even more beautiful, because God delights in the prayers of His children.

"You saw me before I was born. Every day of my life was recorded in your book. Every moment was laid out before a single day had passed." (Psalm 139:16).

Even as a child, I was drawn to Him. My journey of faith began when I was about three years old, living with the Kelly's, members of Pilgrim Rest Baptist Church. I joined the choir, wearing my little black skirt and white shirt, singing songs about a God I did not yet understand. It was the beginning of a love story; one I could not fully comprehend at the time but was already unfolding in the most beautiful and unexpected ways.

When I returned to live with my mother, we lived next to an older Christian couple who would take us to church on Sundays. It was there, at the age of seven, that I first memorized the 23rd Psalm. The words: "The Lord is my shepherd; I have all that I need. He lets me rest in green meadows; he leads me beside peaceful streams" were written in my heart before I even realized how much I would lean on them in the years to come.

As a child, I was a very quick learner, a "copycat" of sorts, memorizing prayers and following the dance of faith I saw in others. But even then, God was guiding me. I may not have known Him, but He knew me. "I knew you before I formed you in your mother's womb. Before you were born, I set you apart…" (Jeremiah 1:5). I was too young to comprehend that this was His love at work, drawing me to Him, nurturing my spirit even when I was incognizant.

The most extraordinary truth about this love story is that it was not I who sought Him first—it was He who loved me first. Long before I was perceptive, God was already walking beside me, shaping my path, waiting for me to grow into the fullness of our relationship. Through every moment of my childhood, every prayer uttered in innocence, His love was steadfast and patient.

Looking back, I can see how He allowed me to grow and develop, not forcing understanding upon me but waiting until the right time to reveal Himself in deeper ways. His love is patient like that, willing to wait, willing to guide, and always there, even when we are oblivious of His presence. As children, we often fail to fully grasp the depth of our relationship with our Heavenly Father, test His love remains steadfast, and He relentlessly pursues us.

Reflection:

As you reflect on the beginnings of your own journey with God, I encourage you to think back to your earliest memories of faith, no matter how simple or small they may seem. Perhaps you, too, learned a bedtime prayer or memorized a Bible verse, not fully understanding its meaning. But it is comforting to know that even when we did not quite grasp who God was, He knew us intimately?

This chapter reminds us of the innocence of childhood faith, where our hearts are open, even if our understanding is still growing. It speaks to the beauty of a God who listens, even when our prayers are mere whispers in simple, childlike words. And it shows that no matter how early or how late we come to know God, He has been with us all along, watching over us, guiding us, and patiently waiting for the right moment to reveal more of His love.

Think about the moments in your own life where God may have been working behind the scenes, drawing you closer to Him even when you were not fully aware. Whether it was through the kindness of others, the words of a song, or the recitation of Scripture, God has always been at work in your story, too.

Faith is a journey—a love story that begins long before we realize it. God does not wait for us to have perfect understanding; instead, He meets us right where we are, whether we are children learning to pray or adults seeking deeper connection. His love is patient, waiting for us to grow into the fullness of our relationship with Him.

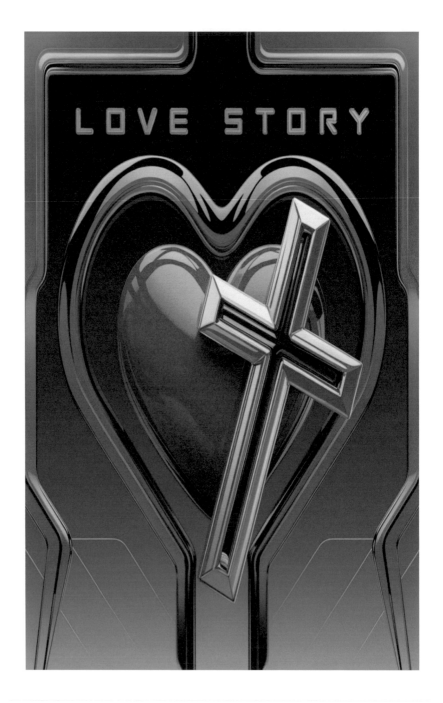

Chapter 2: A Miracle in the Making

Before I could walk, talk, or even understand who God was, His love for me was already at work, shaping my life and extending His grace in ways I could not comprehend. I was born with a painful hernia, a condition that caused me to cry constantly. My mother was led to Dr. Martin Wyngarden, who said if I could gain enough weight, I would be able to undergo surgery to remove the hernia. But for a while, that seemed impossible.

It was then that God, in His divine love, sent an angel to my grandmother's house. She was extremely distressed, watching me suffer in pain, unsure of what to do. But this angel brought with them a message of hope. *"Stop crying,"* the angel said, *"and feed her mashed potatoes with your pinky finger."* And that is exactly what my grandmother did. Slowly but surely, I gained the weight needed for surgery. The pain eased, and my body, though I was too young to remember it, was the recipient of a miracle. "For he will order his angels to protect you wherever you go" (Psalm 91:11).

Looking back now, I see that it was not just a random occurrence or luck. It was the love of God, orchestrating every detail, extending my life, and making a way for me even when I did yet know Him. As an infant, I could not comprehend this miracle. But now, I recognize that it was God's sovereign power at work. His love for me was so great that He moved heaven and earth to ensure I would grow and fulfill the purpose He had planned for me. This reminds me of what the Bible says in Isiah 44:2, "I am your Creator. You were in my care even before you were born."

I often wonder why God would love me so much, even when I could not possibly earn it. The answer is simple: I am His child. He loved me before I was born, and He predestined my life and its purpose long before I took my first breath. His love is unconditional, not something I could ever work for or deserve. "Even before he made the world, God loved us and chose us in Christ to be holy and without fault in his eyes" (Ephesians 1:4).

I grew up a happy child, despite living in a household where love was not freely given. My mother did not profess to be a Christian, and neither of my parents attended church or expressed affection the way I longed for. My birth father was not present, and I later came to realize he might not have even known I was his daughter. However, my stepfather was absent and not involved in my upbringing. Yet, in the absence of my parents' love, I was wrapped in the love of my Heavenly Father.

"Though my father and mother forsake me, the Lord will receive me" (Psalm 27:10). It was God's grace that filled the void. He became my protector, my guide, and my provider. His love surrounded me, giving me the capacity to love even those who could not love me in return. That is the mystery of His grace—it allowed me to survive the deepest obstacles of my life, including being separated from my mother at just three years old and placed in foster care, surviving sexual violence, and becoming a teenage mother at fourteen.

By seventeen, I was living in my own apartment, trying to navigate life with the challenges and burdens that seemed far too heavy for someone so young. But through it all, God's love was with me, holding me together. "My grace is all you need. My power works best in weakness" (2 Corinthians 12:9.)

In hindsight, I can understand that even in those moments of hardship, God was still crafting our love story. His love did not shield me from every trial, but it carried me through each one. As I reflect on those early years, I believe that it was His hand in every detail, guiding me even when I did not recognize it.

As a teenager, I attended church with Moms Freeman. I remember sitting in services, bored and disconnected. The preacher's words seemed distant and out of reach. There was no Sunday school for the youth like me, and the language of the Bible was foreign to my ears. It was during those Sunday services that God was planting seeds in my heart. Those testimonies from the adult members of the congregation, the old hymns, and the scripture readings were all part of the process of drawing me closer to Him. "The seed that fell on good soil represents those who hear and accept God's word and produce a harvest..." (Mark 4:20). Even though I was too immature to understand it at the time.

God was using every moment, every experience to strengthen our relationship. The seeds of faith, planted in those quiet moments of listening, would one day bear fruit. Our love story was still unfolding, even when I could not discern it.

Reflection:

As you reflect on this chapter, consider the ways in which God's hand has been present in your life, even in the moments when you could not fully understand or recognize His love. Sometimes, miracles happen quietly, behind the scenes, through small acts of grace that we do not realize until we look back.

This chapter reminds us of God's tender care, His ability to send help through unlikely sources, and God's deep, unconditional love for us. Even as infants, before we can speak or know Him, God is actively at work in our lives, preparing us for the future He has already planned. He intervenes in miraculous ways, not because we have earned it, but simply because we are His children.

Reflect on your own story—those moments where you now see God's hand, the miracles you may considered good luck at the time. His love for us is not bound by our understanding; it extends beyond what we can see or comprehend. Let this chapter be a reminder that God's grace surrounds us, and His love works through both the visible and invisible moments of our lives, shaping our path toward His purpose.

Chapter 3: The Discovery of Identity

Early in life I was often told I was bright. Eventually, I came to believe it myself and went on to graduate cum laude with my Associate, Bachelor, and Master's degrees. It was a label I accepted, but never fully grasped. My mother's constant moves—from apartment to apartment, city to city, and even across state lines — forced me to adjust quickly. School became a place where I found my footing. I did not necessarily see myself as particularly smart; I simply followed the classroom rules and did what was expected of me. Today, I must acknowledge that God uniquely designed me to thrive academically, even amidst instability.

"For we are God's masterpiece. He has created us anew in Christ Jesus, so we can do the good things he planned for us long ago" (Ephesians 2:10). I often gravitated toward the A's on my report cards and the stars on my papers. They gave me a sense of validation, my confirmation of who I thought I was. I searched for my identity in achievements, not yet realizing that my true identity was rooted in who God is. In retrospect, I wish I knew that my reliance was not on the affirmation of my teacher or anyone else to acknowledge I was smart or good enough—God had already declared that over my life. I was His creation, fearfully and wonderfully made. "Thank you for making me so wonderfully complex! Your workmanship is marvelous—how well I know it" (Psalm 139:14).

My Heavenly Father is a King, which makes me a princess. If only I had grasped that truth, when I was younger, how differently my life might have unfolded. I often wonder if my desire for recognition was truly mines or my mother's, who entered me in talent shows where I just naturally gravitated toward the acknowledgment and praise. Perhaps if I would not have known then what I know now, I would not have felt the need to seek validation from others—to perform for applause and approval. God's love was always present, and His approval was all that truly mattered.

He had already declared my worth long before anyone else did. I am His, crafted by His own hands and given the breath of life. "But you are not like that, for you are a chosen people. You are royal priests, a holy nation, God's very own possession" (1 Peter 2:9).

I loved to dance, not just for the joy of it, but for the applause. Every step I took, every twirl, was a bid for validation. Yet, God was watching over me the whole time, not judging me for my need to belong, but loving me in the way only a perfect Father could. God created me in His image, with all the splendor and glory He intended. The applause I sought was already mine—God was and is proud of me simply because I am His work, His masterpiece. "The Lord your God is with you, the Mighty Warrior who saves. He will take great delight in you; in his love he will no longer rebuke you but will rejoice over you with singing" (Zephaniah 3:17).

As our love story grew, God watched me blossom into the person He created me to be. He patiently waited for me to fully walk in my identity and understand the depth of His love for me. Now, as I grow older, I grasp more of what it means to be His child. I think of how a parent adores their infant, watching with joy as they learn and grow. And though nothing surprises God, He delights in seeing me make choices that reflect my love for Him, acknowledging His presence in my life. "See how very much our Father loves us, for he calls us his children, and that is what we are" (1 John 3:1).

God, you are amazing. I love you more deeply now than ever before. I have not always understood you, but as I learn more about you each day, my love for you grows stronger. You have been with me through every step, shaping me and loving me long before I knew how to return your love. Our love story continues, and I am forever grateful for your grace, your patience, and your never-ending love.

As I continued to grow, so did my understanding of God's love for me. In school, my perception was that my success meant that I received the approval of others, but in reality, my worth is and was always anchored in God. Every good grade, every achievement, was proof of the gifts He had placed in me. And while the world might have applauded my efforts, I have grown to understand that it was God's pleasure to see me flourish in what He had already ordained for me. God's Word reminds me that He was always guiding me, even when I did not realize it:

"The Lord directs the steps of the godly. He delights in every detail of their lives. Though they stumble, they will never fall, for the Lord holds them by the hand" (Psalm 37:23-24).

Every time I adjusted to a new school or a new city, I was not just moving geographically; I was being moved closer to understanding my true purpose in God. In those moments of uncertainty, I relied on my natural ability to adapt. But it was God who gave me the strength to face each change, each challenge, and to do so with resilience. I understand now that every transition, every new situation, was preparing me for a deeper walk with Him.

When I think of how I sought approval through dancing, it reminds me of how much I longed to be noticed and appreciated. The applause filled a temporary need, but it was never enough. What I truly needed was the affirmation that only God could provide. The beauty of God's love is that He finds joy in who I am, not because of my performance, but because I am His creation. In His eyes, I was already more than enough. As the psalmist says, "You made all the delicate, inner parts of my body and knit me together in my mother's womb. Thank you for making me so wonderfully complex! Your workmanship is marvelous—how well I know it" (Psalm 139:13-14).

As I grow in my understanding of God's love, I see that my achievements, my talents, and my outward expressions of success were never the foundation of my identity. Instead, my true identity has always been rooted in being a child of God, a reflection of His love and creativity. Now, when I think of God watching over me, it is as if He is both the creator and the loving parent, marveling at the child He made.

God has never stopped working in my life. Through every stage, He has been shaping me, molding me into the person I am today. And though I often tried to find my worth in the eyes of others, God has shown me that His approval is all I will ever need. His love is unconditional, unwavering, and eternal.

Reflection:

As you reflect on your own journey, how often have you sought validation from the world around you? We chase approval, applause, and accolades, believing they define our worth. But the truth is, no earthly praise can ever measure up to the love and affirmation God has for us.

In school, I tied my value to my successes—the good grades, the awards, the performances. I craved the recognition, thinking it would fill the void inside. But looking back now, I realize that every achievement was not a testament to my worth, but rather to the gifts God placed within me. While the world may have applauded, it was God who delighted in me—not for what I accomplished, but for who I am as His beloved creation.

Perhaps you have felt the same pull, the need to be seen, heard, or admired. But God wants to remind you that you are already enough. You were enough before the applause and you are still enough after the applause fades. His love for you is constant, rooted in the simple fact that you are His.

Every step of your journey, whether in success or in struggle, has been directed by Him. Even in your uncertainty, He has been holding your hand, guiding you closer to His heart. God delights in you, just as you are, and His approval is the only one that will ever truly matter.

Chapter 4: Dreams and Divine Protection

When you are young, you think you have everything figured out. You believe that the world is at your feet and that you have plenty of time to explore it. But life has a way of humbling you, revealing how little you know and how precious each moment truly is. I remember a particularly harrowing experience: the stove in my apartment exploded. My son was sitting right there in the kitchen, and for years, I attributed his survival to my boyfriend at the time who managed to save him.

But now, with the wisdom and clarity that comes from walking with God, I realize that it was God's love that saved my son. He was watching over us, just as He always has. "For He will order His angels to protect you wherever you go. "They will hold you up with their hands, so you won't even hurt your foot on a stone" (Psalm 91:11-12). At that time in my life, strange things began to happen. I started having dreams—vivid, unsettling dreams that felt like premonitions. Some were warnings about future events, while others seemed like distorted reflections of things that had already happened.

One dream in particular was so close to reality that it shook me to my core. I remember being pregnant at the time and asking the doctors if my unborn child could be possessed because I did not understand why I was having these visions. But God was beginning to awaken something deep within me. I lacked the awareness of what was occurring then, but He was revealing one of the gifts He had given me: the gift of dreams.

"In the last days, God says, I will pour out my Spirit upon all people. Your sons and daughters will prophesy, your young men will see visions, and your old men will dream dreams" (Acts 2:17). Back then, I was young, had not yet, surrendered my life to Christ, and knew nothing about spiritual gifts or how God communicates with His children. Every night, I dreamt, and every morning I shared those dreams with my mother and others. People were astonished, often asking, "Do you dream every night?" They found it hard to believe that I could remember such vivid details, but God was using this gift in my life even before I fully understood it.

Over the years, I have had dreams about family members, friends, and even situations I could not explain. I vividly remember a conversation with my youngest brother before he passed. After we hung up, I prayed, but now I realize that what I thought was a prayer was actually a premonition—God preparing me for what was to come. It was not just a random occurrence; it was His way of revealing His plans to me through dreams. "It is the same Holy Spirit who distributes, activates, and operates these different gifts as he chooses for each believer" (1 Corinthians 12:11).

God, in His wisdom and love, gives different gifts to each of His children. To some, He gives the gift of healing, to others, prophecy. For me, He chose the gift of dreams. My dreams occur when I sleep, with my mind and spirit determining the content, message, and timing of when I am presented with a vision or revelation. As a mature Christ follower, I have learned to embrace this gift as a part of my spiritual connection with Him.

Most nights, my dreams are simple, harmless reflections of the day, but there are times when I wake up with a sense of urgency, knowing that God has shown me something significant. I document my dreams immediately upon waking to ensure I do not lose the vision or the message. allowing me to reflect and fully grasp what I experienced. I then pray over the dreams and deliver the message to the person identified as the intended recipient in my dream.

At first, I questioned why God had entrusted me with this gift. It did not feel like a blessing—it felt like a burden. I did not want to dream about things beyond my control or ability to change. But over time, I have come to realize that this is God's way of communicating with me. When I sleep, my soul connects with Him on a deeper level, free from the distractions of the world. During those still and unguarded moments, God reveals insights about the people I love, situations that require prayer, and even truths about myself.

"The Lord our God has secrets known to no one. We are not accountable for them, but we and our children are accountable forever for all that He has revealed to us, so that we may obey all the terms of these instructions" (Deuteronomy 29:29). Now, I perceive my dreams are not a curse but a divine encounter with the one and only true God. It is His way of drawing me closer to Him, of showing me His plans and purposes. What a loving God He is—one who wastes not even a single moment to connect with His child, even in the quiet of the night.

Reflection:
As you reflect on this chapter, take a moment to think about the times in your life when you believed you had everything under control—when you thought you were the one steering the course of your own journey. Have there been moments where, looking back, you now realize that something greater was at work? Maybe it was a narrow escape, a strange coincidence, or even a quiet nudge in your spirit that could not be explained.

Consider the areas of your life where God might be speaking to you, even if you do not fully understand it yet. Are there experiences or dreams that seem significant but leave you feeling uncertain? These may be God's way of communicating with you, inviting you into a deeper relationship with Him.

How often do we miss the divine whispers because we are too focused on our own plans, our own understanding? What would happen if we paused to see those moments of uncertainty or fear as invitations from God—opportunities to trust that He is always watching over us, guiding us, and revealing His purpose, even when we cannot make sense of it in the moment?

God works in mysterious ways, and sometimes it takes time, distance, or a deepening of faith to see His hand at work. I encourage you to reflect on your own life and ask: where might God be revealing His love, protection, and purpose, even when it seems unclear? How can you lean into those moments and trust that He is with you, shaping you, and guiding you on a path that leads to greater understanding and peace?

Chapter 5: From Titles to Names

As we grow develop closer relationship to others, we often create nicknames—distinctive names that capture the essence of our special bond with them. Growing up, some folks called me "Skinny Minnie" because of my small frame. I called my husband "Baby," "Honey," "Sugar Plum," and "Rashardee." These names were personal and reflected the bond we shared. I never called him a handyman because, truth be told, he preferred to pay someone else rather than attempt to fix things himself! Our names for each other evolve as our relationships deepen, moving from formal titles to names born out of love and experience.

In much the same way, that our relationship with others deepen over time, my relationship with God has evolved, leading to the unique names I call Him. In my youth, I referred to Him by the common titles' others used - God, Jesus, Lord, Savior, Yahweh, Elohim, El-Shaddai, and Father. These names are indeed holy and revered, and they have always held true. However, as I have journeyed through life with Him, I have discovered new names that resonate with the ways He has personally intervened in my life. "Let them praise your great and awesome name. Your name is holy!" (Psalm 99:3).

When I needed medical care, God guided my grandmother to the treatment plan that prepared me for the lifesaving hernia surgery. Now, I refer to Him as "The Great Physician." "He heals the brokenhearted and binds up their wounds" (Psalm 147:3). When I required legal assistance, He showed up in the courtroom, granting me favor, earning Him the title "My Advocate." "For the LORD is our judge, our lawgiver, and our king. He will care for us and save us" (Isaiah 33:22).

In moments of scarcity, when I worried about how to feed my children, He provided sustenance. Thus, I call Him "My Provider." "And this same God who takes care of me will supply all your needs from his glorious riches, which have been given to us in Christ Jesus" (Philippians 4:19).

During a time when I was seeking shelter, and even the realtor deemed it improbable, God made a way. Consequently, I refer to Him as "My Way Maker." "I will even make a way in the wilderness, and rivers in the desert" (Isaiah 43:19). Throughout the darkest moments of my life, He has provided me comfort. After losing my mother, my husband, and my siblings, and others close to me He enveloped me in His embrace. "God is our refuge and strength, always ready to help in times of trouble" (Psalm 46:1). He has been my confidant—guarding my secrets and my greatest cheerleader, always reminding me that I am loved.

This love story compels me to recognize all that He has been to me, deepening my understanding of His love. He has been my Father, Mother, Friend, Doctor, Provider, Lawyer, Way Maker, Miracle Worker, Promise Keeper, Light in the darkness, and my All. "For unto us a child is born, unto us a son is given... and His name shall be called Wonderful, Counselor, The Mighty God, The Everlasting Father, The Prince of Peace" (Isaiah 9:6). God embodies all these roles and more because His love for me knows no bounds.

He has also been my protector. I recall a moment in Africa when I believed a semi-truck was heading directly towards the van I was traveling in. In my fear, I cried out, "Lord Jesus!" and we avoided a collision. Another time, a car hit struck me while I was riding my electric bike and I called out His name and walked away with only a scratch. "The name of the Lord is a strong fortress; the godly run to him and are safe" (Proverbs 18:10). He is my shield, my refuge, and my miracle worker.

Reflecting on the various names, I now attribute to God, it reveals a different chapter in our love story— one filled with His faithfulness, protection, and provision. Every time I have needed Him, He has shown up in unimaginable ways. "The Lord is my shepherd; I have all that I need" (Psalm 23:1). What do you call Him? Each of us shares a unique love story with God, and the names and titles we identify Him by reflects how He has revealed His goodness in our lives.

For me, He is my Almighty God. He is my Husband, my Carpenter, my Financial Advisor, my Protector, my Jesus, and so much more. As I continue to experience more of His goodness and His presence daily, more names will be revealed to me to describe our relationship. "Those who know your name trust in you, for you, O Lord, do not abandon those who search for you" (Psalm 9:10).

Reflection:

As you reflect on this chapter, think about the unusual ways God has shown up in your life. What names would you call Him based on the moments when He provided, protected, healed, or guided you? Each name we give Him reflects not only who He is but how He has met us in our most vulnerable moments.

Take a moment to consider: What specific times in your life can you look back on and see His hand at work? Perhaps He was your Provider when you did not know how you would make it through a financial struggle, or He was your Comforter during a season of deep loss.

What unique names have you called Him in response to His faithfulness? Reflect on the chapters of your life that are written by His love and care. Just as you might give special names to those closest to you, how has your relationship with God deepened through the ways He has been there for you?

We often overlook these divine encounters, but each one is an opportunity to recognize a new dimension of who God is to us. How might this reflection lead you to a deeper understanding of His love for you? What new name will you call Him today?

Chapter 6: Deepening Love, Growing Faith

"When I was a child, I spoke and thought and reasoned as a child. But when I grew up, I put away childish things" (1 Corinthians 13:11).

In the early stages of my walk with God, my understanding was refreshingly straightforward.. I saw Him as the Creator, my Lord, and guide, but the depth of His love for me was incomprehensible. As a new believer, I often noticed how other congregants held their pastors in such high esteem, filled with love and respect. I remember wondering why they felt so deeply for their pastor and how their admiration connected to their faith.

Then one Sunday, something within me changed. As I sat in church listening to the sermon, I felt an unexpected and profound emotion welling up inside me—so deep that I leaned over to my husband and said, "I think I have fallen in love with Reverend Dr. Clifton Rhodes Jr.." At the time, I did not realize that this powerful feeling was not just admiration for a person; it was my spirit awakening to a deeper love for God. The emotion I felt was directed at Him, even though I lacked the awareness to understand it. While I loved God, I was only beginning to grasp what it meant to be truly in *love* with Him.

That moment stirred within me a longing for a more intimate relationship with God—a yearning to know Him deeply, not just through the lens of sermons and teachings but through a personal connection. As I matured in faith, I realized that God had been drawing me closer to Him all along, patiently waiting for me to discover the vastness of His love.

In 2024, I received a link to a message by Prophet Lovy Elias. Initially intrigued but unsure of what to expect I began listening and soon found myself captivated. Prophet Lovy spoke of a living God in a way that made Him feel so near, so accessible —as though God was closer than my closest friend. For the first time, I believed that God was not distant but right there with me. Prophet Lovy's teachings revealed to me that God's love is not something I must earn or strive for. His love was already mine, despite all my flaws and imperfections.

Through Prophet Lovy's word, I came to understand that my past mistakes, no matter how big or small, did not disqualify me from God's love. As 1 John 1:9 reminds us, "If we confess our sins, he is faithful and just and will forgive us our sins and purify us from all unrighteousness." God's forgiveness was not conditional—it was freely given, and it was not something I needed to carry guilt for once I repented.

Prophet Lovy also spoke about the grace of God in such a way that it opened my heart to a new level of understanding. He explained that, when we reach heaven, we may be surprised to find that the pages recording our sins may be missing some events from our book of life. This revelation filled me with awe and gratitude, reminding me of Hebrews 8:12 "For I will forgive their wickedness and will remember their sins no more." God's grace is so immense that it erases the very things I have held onto, long after God has let them go.

However, this understanding of grace did not give me permission to live carelessly. Rather, it freed me from the weight of guilt, allowing me to walk in the fullness of His love and forgiveness. Knowing that my sins are/were forever forgiven, I shifted my focus on deepening my relationship with God, allowing His love to transform me from the inside out.

Over time, my spiritual journey with God has grown richer and more intimate. I have witnessed the power of His love in new ways, particularly through Prophet Lovy's teachings. He helped me understand that God is still performing miracles, and displaying signs and wonders today, just as He did in biblical times. The Bible stories are not just historical accounts—they are living testimonies that apply to my life today.

One of the most profound realizations in this journey is that God's love is not just for me— it is for everyone. Being a Christ follower means embracing not only the grace that God offers but also the responsibility of sharing that love with others. We are to be an extension of His love in this world, to forgive as He forgives, and to love even those who are difficult to love. "A new command I give you: Love one another. As I have loved you, so you must love one another" (John 13:34).

As I continue to grow in my faith, I find that the more I learn about God, the deeper my love for Him becomes. Each day is a new opportunity to experience. His presence, whether through His word, through prayer, or in the beauty of creation. His love is present in every sunrise, in every moment of peace, and in every breath I take. I see Him working in my life, guiding me, protecting me, and drawing me closer to Him with every step.

One of the greatest gifts of this journey is the realization that God's love is not just for me—it is for everyone. His desire for us is to know Him genuinely, to walk in His power and authority, and to experience the fullness of life He has promised. As I continue to walk with God, I am committed to growing in grace and extending His love to those around me, knowing that this is the true essence of being a follower of Christ.

Reflection:

As you reflect on this chapter, consider how your relationship with God has evolved over time. When you think back on your early faith, how did you understand God? Have there been moments in your life when that understanding deepened, when you saw God not just as an abstract idea but as a personal, loving presence?

This chapter challenges us to recognize how our spiritual maturity transforms our love for God. What began as simple belief often grows into a more intimate connection, as we experience God's grace, forgiveness, and closeness in ways we did not expect. Have you had moments when you realized that God was much nearer than you thought, or that His love was more personal than you imagined?

Think about the role of forgiveness in your life. Have you held on to guilt for mistakes long after God has forgiven you? What would it look like to release that burden and walk in the freedom of His grace? How does understanding the depth of God's forgiveness change the way you live and interact with others? Finally, reflect on your role as an extension of God's love. In what ways can you share the love and grace you have received with those around you? How has God's love transformed you, and how can that transformation be a light to others in your life?

This chapter invites you to explore these questions thoroughly, drawing upon your own experiences with God. What new insights about His love might you discover in this season of your faith journey?

Chapter 7: Perfect in His Grace: Embracing God's Love Through Imperfection

The concept of perfection often feels daunting. I have come to understand that true perfection lies in aligning with God's will and understand His purpose for your life. Yet, that purpose is not always clear. I remember a time when I thought and believed in my heart that God was calling me to share His name with the world. The message was powerful, but I was not entirely sure if I had heard Him correctly. It was period in my life when nothing seemed certain, and hearing God's voice felt distant. When I shared this with those in my inner circle—they dismissed my story, and I began to doubt whether I had truly heard God at all.

Despite this, I have always felt a desire to tell others about Jesus and the significant changes and deliverance He has made in my life. It is this same drive that compels me to write today. I trust that someone on their own journey of faith will read these words and find encouragement, clarity, and the strength to keep trusting in God. Isaiah 55:11 reassured me that God's word never returns void, "It will accomplish all I want it to, and it will prosper everywhere I send it." Even in my doubt, I believed that God was sowing seeds that would one day bear fruit.

My faith journey has not always aligned with the paths of those around me. Some people in my life have walked away from God or turned to other beliefs—this includes my late husband. We met in church, sharing the same Christian faith and a love for Jesus. But over time, his faith began to shift, creating a divide between us. He started questioning long-held traditions like taking communion and even adopted symbols from other faiths. It was heartbreaking.

Our marriage, once built on shared faith, grew strained. Yet, I held fast to Romans 8:38-39, "I am convinced that nothing can ever separate us from God's love…neither our fears for today nor our worries about tomorrow—not even the powers of hell can separate us from God's love." Even as my husband's beliefs changed, I prayed he would return to the truth we once shared before his passing.

At another point of my life, I served as a church administrator. I sensed a strong call to ministry, so I spoke with the church leadership and pursued theology classes. With time, I have come to realize my calling was not tied to formal ministry. It was about leading people to Christ in ordinary moments of life. One such moment was when I led my mother to faith in Christ in December 2012. Knowing that God used me as a vessel to secure her eternity is a memory I will forever cherish.

More recently, two of my grandchildren professed their faith and were baptized in a Michigan lake. Watching their young faith grow brings me profound hope. Proverbs 22:6 resonates deeply with me: "Train up a child in the way he should go, and when he is old, he will not depart from it." I pray their early journey with God blossoms into lifelong devotion.

Now, I comprehend that striving for perfection means stepping out in faith, even when the path ahead is uncertain. It means sharing the gospel beyond the church walls, beyond our immediate circles. My goal is to inspire others, often through social media, knowing that every post reflects my walk with Christ. Matthew 5:16 speaks to this: "Let your light shine before others, that they may see your good deeds and glorify your Father in heaven." Every day presents a chance to live out this verse, to be a vessel of God's love and truth.

Envisioning my love story with God, I see that it is not about appearing perfect, but about allowing His perfect love to transform me within. When I fall, He lifts me. When I doubt, He reassures me. As I grow deeper in faith, it is less about me and more about Him. His light shines through the cracks in my imperfect life. 2 Corinthians 12:9 sums it up perfectly: My grace is sufficient for you, for my power is made perfect in weakness." My life is living proof that God's grace and mercy can transform even the messiest moments into something beautiful.

Reflection:

Have there been moments in your life where you felt unworthy of God's love? How did you overcome those feelings, and in what ways has God shown His grace and love to you despite your imperfections?

Chapter 8: Trusting God's Divine Plan

In life, we often make plans that that align with our desires and dreams, convinced we know what is best for our future. Yet, many of us find ourselves at pivotal moments where God reveals a different—and far greater—path than the one we imagined.

This has been a recurring theme throughout my journey, especially after the loss of my husband. What began as an effort to cope with grief and rebuild my life led me on a deeply spiritual journey of trust and reliance of God's divine provision. After my husband passed, I was overwhelmed by the grief of losing him and the life we had built together.

We had purchased a home, a beautiful place that was meant to be our sanctuary—a house with a large garage and plenty of space for us to grow. I still remember the anticipation and excitement we felt when we finally closed the sale on the house. It was more than just a structure; it was the manifestation of our hard work, dreams, and future plans.

I can still recall the excitement we felt walking through the doors for the first time. The rooms felt like they were filled with hope and new beginnings. We envisioned our lives unfolding in that space—sharing meals, celebrating anniversaries, and making countless memories. But those dreams shattered when I lost him. What was once our home became an overwhelming reminder of the life, we were supposed to share but never would. The house felt empty without him, and every room echoed the loss. I could not bear to stay there anymore.

Amid my grief, I made the difficult decision to sell the house. It was not easy to let go of the place that held so many memories, but I knew I had to move forward. I could not just move to another place— I needed a fresh start This desire for a change and being taken far from the pain led me to a bold decision: to live full time in an RV. It was not just about finding a new home; it was about seeking freedom and healing through a new adventure that would allow me to rebuild my life on my terms.

I began researching RV living during the peak of the COVID-19 pandemic. I spent hours watching YouTube videos, reading articles, and mentally preparing myself for this drastic lifestyle change. The idea of living on the road, with no permanent address and a life filled with uncertainty, was both terrifying and exciting. But I felt to my core, that this was what I needed to do—what God was leading me to do.

Without even considering the fact that I lacked experience living in an RV. I trusted that God would provide what I needed, but I had no idea how He would show up in ways that exceeded my understanding. There were obstacles from the start. For one, I needed a truck powerful enough to tow the RV. The dealerships were all but empty due to supply chain shortages, and finding the right vehicle seemed impossible.

Days turned into weeks, and I began to doubt if this plan would ever come together. Then, one night, I received a call unexpected. A shipment arrived at the dealership, and among the vehicles was a 2022 3500 Diesel RAM dually truck, the exact vehicle I needed. It was no coincidence—God made a way when it seemed impossible. I knew it was a blessing from God. "And my God will meet all your needs according to the riches of his glory in Christ Jesus" (Philippians 4:19).

With the truck secured, I set off for Michigan to purchase the Jayco Northpoint. This was part of my journey of faith, one I was determined to walk despite the unknown ahead. After purchasing the RV, I returned to Phoenix, Arizona, and securing a spot seemed impossible. Phoenix was going to be my home base and landing spot. I was hopeful, but the challenges came almost immediately. In October, I was heading back to Arizona during the height of RV season. Finding a spot at an RV park in Arizona proved almost impossible. After considerable searching, I finally found one park with an available lot on my way back. It was not what I had envisioned, but I trusted God's plan.

While living at that park, I met a woman named Elizabeth. Her story was one of immense heartbreak: her husband, son, and a close friend had all committed suicide within a six-month span. She was struggling deeply, taking care of her six-year-old son while battling her own grief and isolation. It was clear to me that Elizabeth was in a dark place, overwhelmed by depression and self-destruction.

I felt strongly that God had placed Elizabeth in my path for a reason. I knew I was meant to be a light for her during this challenging time in her life. I tried to reach out, inviting her to breakfast, but she declined repeatedly. Despite her initial rejections, I persisted. I sensed that she needed someone, and honestly, so did I. I told her, "We are both widows, and we could support each other through this."

Eventually, Elizabeth began to open her heart to me. Our relationship grew, and I saw it as an assignment from God. My love story with God has always involved stepping into places where His light was needed and, in this moment, I was to be that light for Elizabeth. One day, the storage unit I had been renting raised its prices. I decided that it was time to get rid of 90% of my belongings and donate them to a second-hand store. Elizabeth and her son helped me with this task, each of us driving our trucks to clear out the unit. Elizabeth was shocked at how easily I made the decision to let go of so many things, as she herself had two storage units filled with possessions, she could not bring herself to part with. She asked if I would help her with her storage situation as well.

We went to her unit, but once we arrived, she could not bring herself to let go of any of the items. "They are just too expensive," she said, canceling the plan to downsize. We never went back, and over time, our relationship became strained. I noticed that she had returned to using mind-altering substances, and not long after, I relocated to another RV park.

Through this, I saw that Elizabeth was placed in my life for a season, and while our paths eventually diverged, I passionately believe God used me to plant seeds of hope in her life. Whether or not those seeds ever blossomed was not for me to control—I simply had to trust in God's timing and plan.

One of my greatest challenges was Arizona's s unrelenting heat was one thing, but the technical and mechanical issues with the RV were overwhelming. Despite all my research, nothing prepared me for the reality of life on the road. I lacked the experience to maintain the RV, handle the hookups, or troubleshoot the inevitable mechanical issues that would arise.

But, in God's perfect timing, He sent me help. My neighbor in the RV park, Mike, owned the same model as mine. With years of experience under his belt, Mike took me under his wing and taught me everything I needed to know. From basic maintenance to troubleshooting complicated issues, Mike's guidance was invaluable. It was not just about fixing things; Mike became a friend when I desperately needed one. I can look back now and see that Mike was an instrument of God's provision, placed in my life to guide me through that tough transition.

Mike eventually moved on, as most people do in the transient world of RV living. I was scared at first. Without his expertise, I felt exposed and vulnerable. But I realized something profound: God had used Mike to teach me what I needed to know for that season, and now it was time for me to trust Him more deeply. This was not just about RV living; it was about my faith, learning to lean on God alone when all earthly supports faded away.

Even after Mike left, God continued to send help at the exact moments I needed it. When I moved back to Michigan and encountered electrical issues with the RV that I had no idea how to fix, He sent Ken, an electrician, who showed up right on time. Ken was not just a technician; he was another reminder of how God's provision is constant, even in the smallest details of our lives.

However, as winter approached, I knew the Arizona heat had taken its toll on the RV, and I began to worry if it could manage Michigan's brutal winter. Feeling the urgency to find a permanent place to live before the first heavy snow arrived. I began looking for a house in Michigan. But I was unemployed and finding a house to purchase seemed out of reach. Leasing a home, however, also proved to be a challenge, and after weeks of searching it felt like I was going in circles.

As always, I prayed, and then, God sent another answer. I came across a realtor who had a house listed on the market. When I asked him if the if the owners would consider leasing, he said no, but then offered to help me in my search for something suitable. For the next three weeks, he would send me listings, and I would ask him to reach out to the owners to see if they were willing to lease. The realtor was patient but did not seem too optimistic-perhaps he thought this search would end up in disappointment, and I would eventually give up. But God had other plans.

One evening, the realtor called me and said, "Erma, I have got a builder's home. Would you be interested?" I did not hesitate—I said yes. It was October, and I knew the snow was coming soon. The urgency to find a home before winter was weighing heavily on me. I prayed to God, asking for shelter before the harsh cold arrived. I understood that Michigan winters can be brutal and the temperatures dropping below zero degrees could destroy the RV.

The day the realtor showed me the house, I walked through it, praying silently, "Lord, is this where You want me to live?" As I looked out of the window, I saw flurries—the first sign of snow. In that moment, I knew. God was answering my prayer, showing me that this was where He wanted me to be. The snow was coming, and He had provided just in time. I turned to the realtor and said, "I will take it."

This house was not just a place to live. I knew it was a home built for me by God, and He provided it at exactly when I needed the most. Every detail of the journey—from selling my previous home, living in the RV, and struggling to find shelter—was part of God's greater plan. He had led me here, step by step, always providing exactly what I needed, even when it seemed impossible.

I genuinely believe, this house is a gift from God. It is a constant reminder that no matter what we face, He is the giver of every good thing. My love story with God is not just about the miraculous; it is about the everyday ways He shows up and provides, guiding me through each season of life. His love is constant, His timing is perfect, and He always makes a way. "For I know the plans I have for you," says the Lord. "They are plans for good and not for disaster, to give you a future and a hope" (Jeremiah 29:11).

Reflection:

In life, we often craft plans that reflect our desires and dreams, believing we know what is best for our future. Yet, how often do we find ourselves standing at a crossroads, only to realize that God has a different and more profound purpose in store for us? This truth resonates deeply with my journey of grief, healing, and rediscovery after losing my husband.

As you reflect on your own life, consider the moments when your plans took an unexpected turn. What dreams did you have that crumbled, and how did those moments of loss shape your path forward? It is easy to become consumed by what we have lost, feeling as though our lives have been derailed. But could it be that those moments of surrender are the very spaces where God's grace begins to flourish?

When I made the decision to leave behind my home—a sanctuary filled with memories; I became filled with fear and uncertainty. Yet, in that leap of faith, I discovered a profound truth: sometimes, the most challenging decisions lead us to the most beautiful places. My journey into RV living became a metaphor for shedding the weight of my past and embracing the unknown, guided by a God who provides in ways we cannot always foresee.

Take a moment to think about your own "RV moments." Are there situations in your life where you felt compelled to step away from familiarity in search of healing and hope? How did you witness God's provision in those times? It may not always look like what you expect, but His fingerprints frequently are found in the people with whom enter our lives, the unexpected blessings, and the lessons learned along the way.

In times of despair, I encountered individuals like Elizabeth, whose struggles reminded me of the shared human experience of grief. Consider the people God has placed in your life. Are there relationships that challenge you to step outside of yourself and be a light for others? How can you lean into those connections, even when it feels uncomfortable?

This chapter of my life ultimately taught me that surrendering my plans to God opened the door to experiences far greater than I could have imagined. As you ponder your own journey, reflect on this: How might God be inviting you to trust Him more deeply, to embrace His unexpected path, and to discover the beauty in the unfolding of your story?

Chapter 9: Discovering My True Number One

I previously thought my husband was the number one person in my life. He was my confidant, my companion, and the person I depended on day to day. We shared over 17 years together, and naturally, he became my closest companion. But life also brought me my brother Richard, whom I considered my number two. He was the person I turned to for advice, encouragement, and insight. Richard was not just my brother; he was a close friend, someone who saw me through life's trials and triumphs. Even though he was my younger brother, we had a relationship that felt more like the bond a mother and son have, as our mother could not provide the emotional support, we both needed. His love and care for me, like my husband's, grounded me.

But then, life shifted. I lost my number two—Richard. His passing felt like a piece of me was torn away. Losing him at only 49 years old, when he had so much more to live for, was devastating. I remember how I had just walked through the hospital parking lot, ready to be there for him as I promised during his liver transplant. He made it through that surgery, but his time on earth was cut short a few months later.

When Richard passed, I found myself leaning even more on my husband. His presence helped me navigate the grief of losing my brother. Without realizing it, I had transferred the emotional support I once relied on from Richard to my husband. But then, four years later, I faced another heart-wrenching loss—my husband. Now my number one and my number two were both gone.

I began to question so many things: Who could I turn to now? In this moment of grief, I needed to focus and confront the deeper truth—God had always been my number one. Losing the people I loved the most made me realize that while people come and go, God remains.

"The Lord himself goes before you and will be with you; he will never leave you nor forsake you. Do not be afraid; do not be discouraged" (Deuteronomy 31:8). It was as if I had forgotten that God is a jealous God, as He says in His Word. "For the Lord, whose name is Jealous, is a jealous God" (Exodus 34:14). I placed others in roles that belonged to Him. Only after my number one and number two were gone did I realize that God had always been standing with me, behind me, loving me and waiting for me to fully depend on Him.

In my grief, I now see that God permitted me to go through the losses so I could grow closer to Him. "And we know that in all things God works for the good of those who love him, who have been called according to his purpose" (Romans 8:28). Now, God is not just my number one—He is my all!

Today, I have come to understand that while relationships on earth are important, none should come before my relationship with God. "But seek first the kingdom of God and his righteousness, and all these things will be added to you" (Matthew 6:33).

Reflection:

Who have you ranked as number one in your life? How does your relationship with God fit into that ranking, and how can you seek Him first, even when life challenges your priorities?

Chapter 10: My Love Story with God

What if you had a secret admirer—someone who loved you from the very beginning, even when you did not know it? Imagine this person desiring a relationship with you, constantly drawing you closer, never judging you, waiting patiently, and always working behind the scenes to protect and support you. What if this secret admirer had written you a love letter, expressing His deep affection for you and promising you a place in His mansion, offering you the keys to His Kingdom? Would you say yes?

This is the story of my love affair with God, a love that I did not recognize for so long. Yet, deep within my soul, I longed for something more, even when I did not fully understand what it was. God was always there, waiting for me to come to Him, longing for the moment I would say "yes." "The Lord appeared to us in the past, saying: 'I have loved you with an everlasting love; I have drawn you with unfailing kindness" (Jeremiah 31:3).

I spent years unaware of how deeply He loved me, how much He was with me through every trial, every heartache, and every moment of joy. Even when I could not see Him, did not believe in Him, or did not trust Him, He was always there, drawing me closer to His heart. "You do not realize now what I am doing, but later you will understand" (John 13:7). God was never far away; He was always waiting, loving me from a distance, until I was ready to receive Him fully.

I can now comprehend how the deepest parts of me were always calling out for the deepest parts of Him. "Deep calls to deep in the roar of your waterfalls; all your waves and breakers have swept over me" (Psalm 42:7). There was a longing in my soul for a love that went beyond the physical and the temporary—a love so deep and strong that could only be found in Him. Even when I did not know how to express it, my soul was searching for the One who had been searching for me all along.

God, in His infinite patience and love, waited for me to return to Him. "But God demonstrates his own love for us in this: While we were still sinners, Christ died for us" (Romans 5:8). He did not rush me or push me, but He quietly worked in my heart, tenderly guiding me toward Him, even when I resisted. It took time, but eventually, I came to understand that His love for me is unconditional. There is nothing I can do, nothing anyone else can do, to separate me from His love. "I give them eternal life, and they will never perish. No one can snatch them away from me" (John 10:28).

Now, I know without a doubt that I am loved by God. And guess what? You are too. This love is not just for me; it is for everyone. God has been waiting for you just as He waited for me, drawing you closer to Him with every breath you take. "See how very much our Father loves us, for he calls us his children, and that is what we are!" (1 John 3:1).

This love story is about the journey God, and I have shared, the moments I did not realize He was right there beside me, and the times I resisted, only to find that He was waiting patiently. It is about how I have come to know and experience His love and how, despite everything, He has always been drawing me into a relationship with Him.

God's love for us is deeper than we can imagine. He desires intimacy with us, a relationship that transforms our hearts and lives. He is better than a secret admirer, the One who loved us before we even knew Him, the One who calls us by name and says, "You are mine." "I have called you by name; you are mine" (Isaiah 43:1).

This is our story, and it is just the beginning. I invite you to discover the love God has for you, to embrace the relationship He is offering. He has always loved you, and there is nothing you can do to change that. He waits for you, just as He waited for me, with open arms and a heart full of love.

"Love is patient and kind. Love is not jealous or boastful or proud or rude. It does not demand its own way. It is not irritable, and it keeps no record of being wronged. It does not rejoice about injustice but rejoices whenever the truth wins out. Love never gives up, never loses faith, is always hopeful, and endures through every circumstance" (1 Corinthians 13:4-8).

Welcome to my love story with God—where every chapter reveals a new depth of His grace, mercy, and unending love.

Reflection:

As you reflect on your own journey, consider this: What if the love you have been seeking has been with you all along, patiently waiting, unwavering and unconditional? God's love is not distant or abstract; it is personal, tangible, and eternal. Even when life feels overwhelming or you are uncertain about where to turn, His love is there—quietly calling you closer, ready to embrace you just as you are.

You do not have to earn this love or chase after it; it has been chasing you from the start. In every struggle, every moment of joy, and every breath you take, God has been by your side, drawing you toward Him. Just as He waited for me, He's waiting for you—with arms open wide.

So, if your heart longs for something deeper, for a love that transcends everything else, know that it is already yours. The love God offers is endless, unconditional, and always available. All you need to do is say "yes" and embrace the beautiful relationship He has been offering you all along.

Let this be the beginning of your own love story with God, one that transforms your heart, fills your soul, and draws you into the fullness of His grace. Remember, you are already deeply loved—just as you are.

I am honored to share my "Love Story" with God, as revealed through His Son, Jesus Christ, in this book.

"For this is how God loved the world: He gave his one and only Son, so that everyone who believes in him will not perish but have eternal life. God sent his Son

into the world not to judge the world, but to save the world through him" (John 3:16-17).

This truth is foundational to my faith, and I rest in the assurance of eternal life with God.

May I ask you something**?**

Do you know Jesus?

Today could be the beginning of a profound life change for you:

"If you declare with your mouth, 'Jesus is Lord,' and believe in your heart that God raised him from the dead, you will be saved" (Romans 10:9).

Conclusion: Eternal Love

Every love story has a beginning, but my love story with God is one that has no end. It is a story that stretches beyond time, into eternity. It started with miracles, the discovery of my identity in Christ, divine protection, dreams and visions, the realization of God's perfect grace, and the deepening of my faith. My journey of trusting God's divine plan has shown me that His love is perfect even through my imperfections. I once ranked people in my life as number one, two, and three, but I have now come to understand that God has always been—and will always be—my true number one.

Through the many seasons of my life, God has been constant. When I lost my brother and my husband, I was forced to reckon with the reality that no human love could ever replace the love of God. I came to fully understand that God, who had always been with me, was the only one who would never leave or forsake me. As Psalm 73:26 says, "My flesh and my heart may fail, but God is the strength of my heart and my portion forever." I have learned that in every trial, God's love has been my anchor.

My prayer is that you, too, see how God has been working in your life—how He has been patiently waiting for you to fully turn your heart toward Him. The love of God is unlike any other, and once you experience it deeply, you will understand that nothing in this world can compare. "We know how much God loves us, and we have put our trust in his love. God is love, and all who live in love live in God, and God lives in them." (1 John 4:16).

Reflection:

As we reach the conclusion of this love story with God, I invite you to reflect on your own journey and the profound truths it holds. Just as I discovered that my love story with God is eternal, so too is your relationship with Him. Consider the moments in your life where His love has been evident—through miracles, answered prayers, or the quiet whispers of comfort in your darkest hours.

How has God been your anchor in times of loss, uncertainty, or pain? In what ways has He shown you that His love transcends human relationships and expectations? As you ponder these questions, remember that you are not alone; God's presence is a constant in your life, patiently waiting for you to open your heart fully to Him.

Reflect on the verses that resonate with your experiences. Let them serve as reminders of His unwavering love. Like Psalm 73:26 reminds us, even when we feel weak, "God remains the strength of my heart:" and he is my portion forever. Allow these truths to encourage you to deepen your trust in His divine plan.

Take a moment to consider how you can cultivate this eternal love in your own life. How can you express your gratitude for His presence? How can you share the light of His love with others, just as I attempted to do with Elizabeth? As you embark on the next chapter of your own love story, remember: God's love is perfect, unchanging, and always available to you. Embrace it, cherish it, and let it guide you toward a deeper understanding of your identity in Him. Your journey with God is just beginning, and its significance will echo throughout eternity.

Acknowledgments

First and foremost, I give all honor and glory to God, who is the head of my life. Without His divine guidance and prompting, none of this work would have been possible. I am continually humbled by His unwavering love and direction.

I would also like to express my heartfelt gratitude to the many men and women of God who have poured into my spiritual journey and the unfolding of this *Love Story* with the Lord. I am particularly grateful for Mr. and Mrs. Kelly, Pastor Harvey Hester, Jackie Hester, Dr. Clifton Rhodes Jr., Pastor Artie Lindsay, Mary Freeman, Reverend Dr. Wayne Schmidt, Pastor Kyle Ray, Joyce Meyer, Pastor Steven Furtick, Pastor Jerry Bishop, Pastor Chandler Stevens, Prophet Lovy L. Elias, and countless others. God has used each of you uniquely to advance His Kingdom, and I am blessed to be a beneficiary of your faithful ministries. May you continue to spread the gospel and extend His love throughout the world.

Furthermore, I extend my deepest thanks to Pastor Chris Carroll and the entire team at Life Stream Church for embodying Christ-like leadership and serving as a living example of God's love.

My *Love Story* was inspired by the "Love Actually" series, taught under the guidance of Pastor Chris Carroll, whose teachings encouraged me to boldly share my faith. His message "Kingdom Influencer" series was especially impactful, reminding me of the importance of including the message from Romans 10:9 and the profound truth that "subtle is not enough to save." Each Sunday, our service closes with the powerful reminder: "You are Loved."

To my mother, thank you for sending me to church where I was planted in the Word and taught to treasure scripture through memory verses. Your guidance laid the foundation for my faith, and I am eternally indebted.

Finally, to each reader who holds this book in their hands, thank you for allowing my words to reach your heart. I hope that as you journey through these pages, you are inspired to say "Yes" to the love and truth that only Christ can offer.

Works Cited

Holy Bible. New Living Translation (2015). Bible Gateway. https://www.biblegateway.com (Original work published 1996)

Made in the USA
Columbia, SC
13 November 2024

46275690R00029